from the creator of
Everyone Can Learn [

Look for the
MATH
Around You

FRACTIONS

Alice Aspinall

LOOK FOR THE MATH AROUND YOU: FRACTIONS
Copyright © by Alice Aspinall
First edition 2020

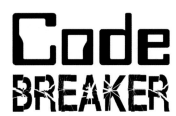

www.codebreakeredu.com

Get the entire

Look for the MATH Around You series!

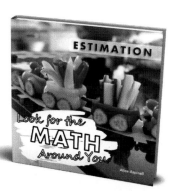

From the Author:

This book features photos taken from everyday, real-life moments. Use the photos as prompts to start a math conversation with children. Each photo is accompanied by optional question prompts. In some cases, there are many correct answers. The thinking process and mathematical discussion are more important than the correct answers. Have fun!

Spread the math love,
Alice ♡

How many equal pieces does the waffle have?

Each piece of the waffle is covered in little squares (and partial squares). Count the squares. Is there an equal amount on each piece of waffle?

How much white do you think is in this photo? How many different ways can you describe your answer?

Try to describe your answer using numbers.

The brownie needs to be shared with 8 people. Show the different ways you can cut the brownie so that all 8 people get the same amount of brownie to eat.

The glass of juice was full before someone drank from it. How much juice has been drank in the photo on the left? Describe your answer using thirds.

How much juice is left in the glass in the photo on the right? How can you describe this amount using a fraction?

How many slices has this pizza been cut into?

Your friend eats three slices of the pizza. How much pizza did they eat? Can you describe this as a fraction of the whole pizza? What other fraction can you use to describe the amount of pizza your friend ate?

Another friend eats three slices of the pizza. How much pizza is left now? What fractions can you use to describe this amount?

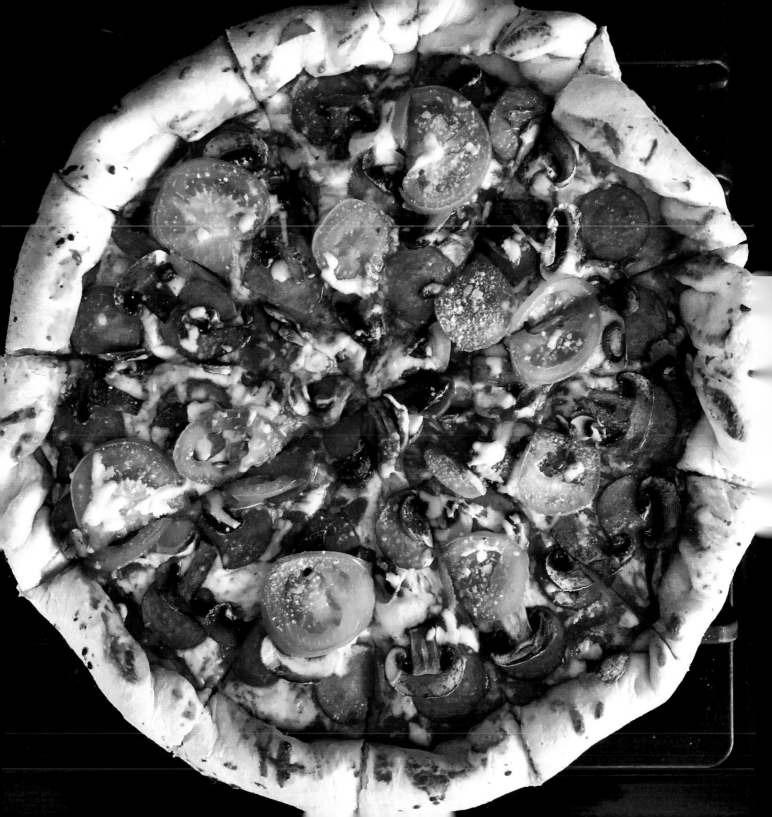

How many bowling pins are in the photo?

How many of the pins are white?

How many of the pins are light blue?

Compare the number of white pins to light blue pins.

What fraction of the total pins are light blue? How else can you express this fraction?

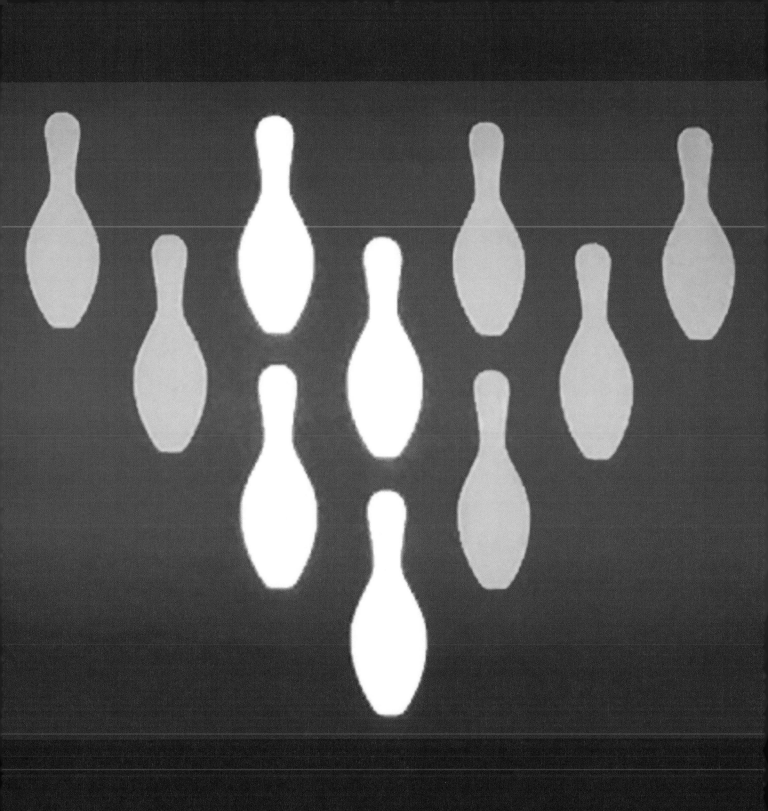

How many circles are in the dough?

You use two of the circles to make pies. What fraction of the circles did you use?

If we take the three circles out, how would you describe the amount of left over dough?

How much of the quesadilla is missing? Can you describe the amount as a fraction of the entire quesadilla?

Imagine the quesadilla had been cut into four large equal pieces instead. How many of these smaller slices would be in each large piece?

Use fraction language to answer the questions:

How much of the drawing is blue?

How much of the drawing is purple?

How much of the drawing is white?

The four photos of bread show different ways the bread can be cut. Point out the two photos that show bread cut into equivalent portions. Describe how these are cut.

How would you describe the cuts made on the other two pieces of bread? Use words and use fraction language to describe the cuts.

The cookie in the photo needs to be split up into six equal parts. We accidentally cut it as you see in the bottom right photo. How can you fix the cookie to make sure we get six equal pieces?

The image shows blankets and pillows on shelves.

What fraction of the pillows are yellow?

What fraction of the blankets are white?

The top photos show measuring cups. Match the fractions to the cups by looking at their size:

$\frac{1}{2}$ cup $\frac{1}{4}$ cup   **1** cup $\frac{1}{3}$ cup

The bottom photos show measuring spoons. Match the fractions to the spoons by looking at their size:

$\frac{1}{2}$ tsp   **1** tbsp $\frac{1}{4}$ tsp   **1** tsp

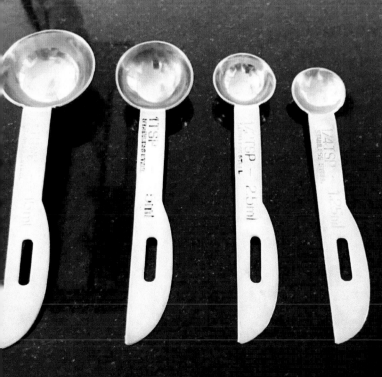

How many squares are black?

How many squares are white?

What fraction of the chess board is black? What fraction is white? What do you notice?

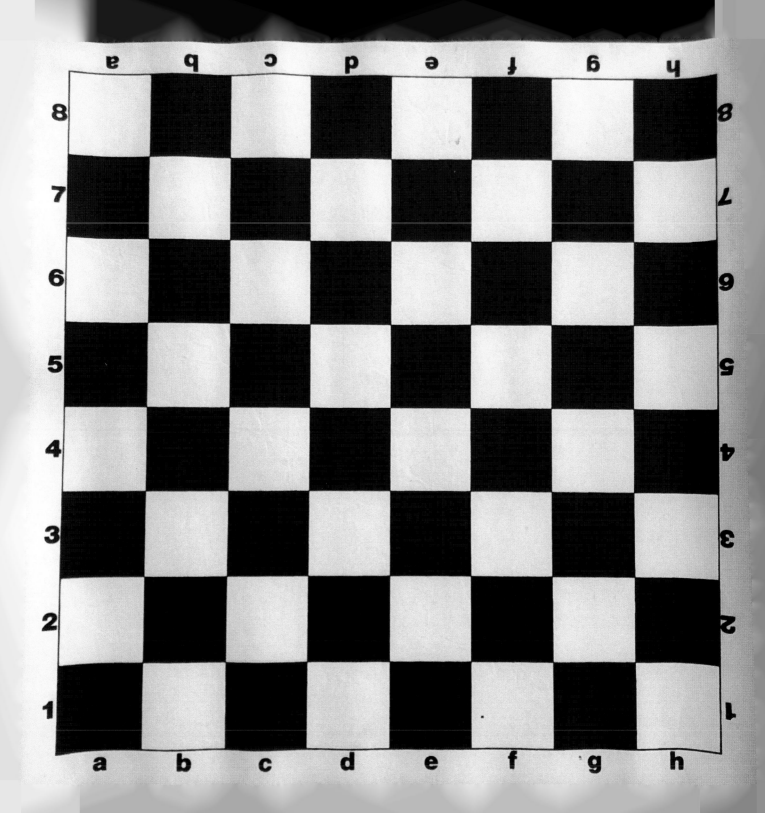

How many rock climbing holds do you see?

What fraction of the holds are yellow? How can you state that fraction a different way?

What fraction of the holds are blue?

What fraction of the holds are blue and pink?

The cup on the left of the photo is filled with flour. This is a $\frac{1}{2}$ cup measuring cup. The cup on the right is a 1 cup measuring cup. How many of these $\frac{1}{2}$ cups would be needed to fill the cup on the right?

The spoon at the bottom of the photo is a $\frac{1}{2}$ teaspoon measuring spoon. How many of these would make 1 whole teaspoon?

The block of butter at the top of the photo is 2 cups of butter. How many $\frac{1}{2}$ cup measuring cups could you fill with this butter?

Estimate how many pumpkins there are in total. Then, count the pumpkins.

Estimate how many pumpkins are white. Then, count the white pumpkins. Compare the number of white pumpkins to the total number of pumpkins. Write this comparison as a fraction.

Choose another kind of pumpkin in the photo. How many of this pumpkin are in the photo? Describe the amount as a fraction of the total pumpkins.

You and four friends would like to share the lollipops. How many lollipops should each of you get?

What fraction of the total lollipops do you each get? Is there another way to say this fraction?

Count the eggs.

How many eggs would be in half of the pan?
Describe how you know.

How many eggs would be in a quarter of the pan?
Describe how you know.

How can you use fractions to describe how much of each colour is in this photo?

Estimate how much of the photo is covered by each colour

Count the books in the tallest stack.

Estimate what fraction of all the books is in the tallest stack.

Count all of the books on the table. How close is your estimate of the books in the tallest stack?

Estimate how many treats are in the photo.

How much of the photo do you think is bags of chips/crackers?

Choose a treat. How many of that treat are in the photo? What fraction of all the treats is this amount?

Alice Aspinall, B.Math(Hon), B.Ed, is a Portuguese-Canadian secondary mathematics educator in Ontario, Canada. She loves spending time with her husband and two children reading books, playing math games, and exploring the outdoors.

Alice is a strong advocate of the growth mindset. She is continually looking for ways to build young people's confidence in math and to make math fun, challenging, and satisfying. Her innovative lessons and her dedication in the classroom have made a positive impact on her students' attitudes toward math. Her YouTube channel, "MrsALovesMath," exemplifies her commitment to her students' learning.

Alice is also a champion for females in STEM by encouraging girls to pursue science and mathematics both in high school and in post-secondary education.

Alice believes everyone can learn math and she is on a mission to prove it.

Alice is also the author of children's books, *Everyone Can Learn Math* and *Let's Explore Math*.

Look for the Math Around You: Fractions is a collection of real-life photos with question prompts to help start math conversations with children. Fractions appear in many ways in our lives — not just in the classroom. Explore the countless places we can find fractions in our world. Perfect for reading at home or in the classroom, this book will help children see math in their daily lives. Use the optional prompts or go off-script and have fun looking for the math around you!

www.everyonecanlearnmath.com

CODE BREAKER PRACTICAL SERIES

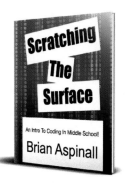

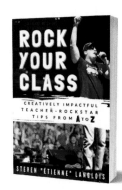

CODE BREAKER LEADERSHIP SERIES

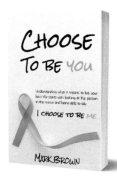

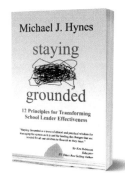

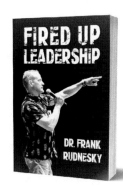

CODE BREAKER KID COLLECTION

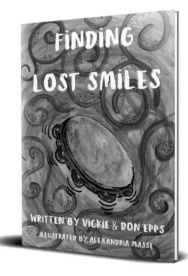

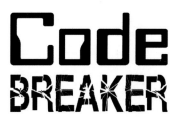

www.codebreakeredu.com